THESE ARE WORDS

COLLECTION OF POEMS

ATHARVA HANMALWAR

Made with ♥ on the Notion Press Platform
www.notionpress.com

Contents

Contents

Contents

Contents

Discription

These book consists of space theories, Stardust, nature , history of wars, empires , quotes , cities and many more;

You will see the dazzling elements related to Cosmos and space

.

The life is related to college and student life.

There is the poems based on thousands of emotions;

You can correlate the poem with your daily life and college life of youngsters;

The book consists of soldiers poem too having inspiration for the sake of country and nationalism spirit;

Having poems related to winter, autumn and shades of seasons;

With kingdoms, connections , world war , Titan and lot more too read;

Heal yourself

Just relax , heal yourself first,

No need to panic or destroy yourself by overthinking,

Just close your eyes, and listen to the inner soul of your universe,

The soul will tell you make perfect move,

To be a good future ;

About The Author

Atharvahanmalwar is from Chandrapur, Maharashtra. He is poet, writer and storyteller. He had created stories.

He is basically passionate towards rap music. He has recently published his 1ˢᵗ debut book " A star is reborn". These is a special book consists of various new elements of life and revolution in society.

He dedicated his book to his father and Mother.

Without there support the book can't be finished.

The most supportable people and entire family made equal contribution of my life.

So I dedicate these book to my family.

And special thanks to my mom, who always with me as friend to complete the book.

These book consists of journey of seasons,

You have to move forward from obsession in life to further.

These book consists of language of fire which express through poetry to change the society;

Life is never on smooth sail and sometimes it goes tough you have to move further.

It consists of various war, college life and day to day goes in life.

He is further coming with again new poem and novel which consists of new shades on life.

1. Perspectives

Some people are born with tornadoes in their lives,
But constellations in their eyes, other people are born with stars
at their feet to fly high,
But their souls are lost at the sea,
These people are like lemonades of emotions,
But still wonderful breathe in their lives;
But still wonderful breathe in their lives,
Some are the beauty angels of life,
With hope, they learn with perspectives;

2. The peace

I find peace near the river side, were the white daffodils grow;
I find peace in the night sky, were you seen like the moon, in the
night sky,
I find peace in the lonely road , were birds and little squirrel
make noise and silent roads,
I find the peace at the bird sanctuary were the wildlife leave,
I find peace in the mountains were mother goddess spell the
truth,
I find peace near the ocean, which shows reflections of tide, and
your inner soul,
I find life , being path of the lonely one,
To move further without anger and endemity,
With peace you have to flow silently;
Quote:-
Our life is a journey on a long and straight road that will lead
you to success

3. A Remainder from smaller being

The bird building her home on your windowsill had every nest
destroyed before;
The spider that is delicately weaving a silken masterpiece has
every single thread broken before;
And despite it all, they try again,
Again to build there nest of dream home,
You no, to broke the home, is entirely easy,
But to build home it needs , hardwork and efforts to fulfill the
dream;

4. Experience of Life

The life teaches you, sometimes starve you, afraid you, end you;
Respite of Happiness, and joy,
It again pulled you back to the danger zone,
Were you struggle, strife , hesitate but thou,
You failed;
You are at the last hope of your day,
To resist it, with last breathe,
But clouds sprinkles the rain, with showering the Stardust to
your hand,
To get magical world, were you are happy and enjoyable with
your buddies;
The conjunctions, of life changes to interjections ;
With lots of rejections, from sea birds ,
Again starting from perspectives , to the edge of confection ;

5. Being Graduate

You love your friends, your destiny and your dream,
But you lost your friends at the end,
You certified for your jobs, and placements too ;
What about the old one;
They change there way, everybody departs from the hostels ,
With backpack ready for the new destiny;
Were new friends, new job , new phone;
We captured the old memories in hostels , but what about next?
Our life goes from 20's to 25's and more,
But the memories get imprinted in our mind,
Those days were memorable, never come back again;
But still with heavy Heart we goes from the college;
Enter to new world with maturity and lot of experience about
all;
We got graduates with flying hats, that's the life gives you a flying
colours to spread around the world;
We are beautiful,
You hold my hand, for lifetime
We floats as changing water,
We washed the stems
We tried our best to preserve this
But like lilies, in a vase

We remain in that space called between neither in love nor out
of it,
A time will come when we decay let me hold your hand
Let us spend a time ,
With ocean & tides
As beautiful one ;

6. Dark Day

I was left alone near the tunnel, were the clinched of leaves and
the cross were flying around and round,
The dark clouds were lightening and the rain get drizzling high,
The leaves were weaving in air,
No lights, just dark night with lightening occurs,
There was the tunnel were one train is coming,
With light scattering on the floor,
It was the dark day, Were nothing is there ;

7. Salt and sugar

The things is still I believe it, the sky during the thunder;
The sea during the storm,
The earth during its dark hours,the sun does not abondon us
when a storm visits,
The sea does not abandon the cliffs because they are hardened to
touch;
I am asking you to hold yourself that is need of more love;

8. The price

Ask anyone who walks on the earth,
And most will say they just want a peaceful life;
A hug from someone they care for,
A warm bed to sleep in , a home filled with love,
A lot of laughter and someone to share a drink with,
At the end it is the people who pay for the carnage,
The mother who must bury her children,
The father who never comes back home,
The sister who will never know the joy of a shared meal again,
The friends lost along the way,
The sky lost the clouds, the any lost there home,
The sea changes the waves , the sun rise through the west,
A thousands of homes wrecked and a million memories
shattered,
All because someone else decided to send a war to knock down
their door,

9. Message to the Universe

In every moments of your existence, several relatives,
Are bursting across the cosmos, planet explodes , stars bursts,
Solar system dissolves in the loop of blackhole,
Welcome a new planet into the orbit of their own sun like star,
The universe gives them life and says now help me live,
Listen, I am saying that if you change your thoughts,
You,too can change the message of the universe;

10. It's 2022

Everyone settling up, rising up from breaking down,
Has broken down or has left more tragedies,
The cosmos truly intends for a person to feel,
And it's hard to say , this shall pass
We are rising high from the pandemic,
Growing from world to universe ,
We are ready with leading the path of success ,
Were no descends , just powerful play should start to win as
victory;

11. Space

You're carved it for so long, that you are overwhelmed by it,
Maybe not for the first day, away from the home,
But though the outer universe, I see the earth, as tiny lights and
blinking,
Were there is my home, I miss my mom and my dad too ??
They also miss you as you do.
You see the home but I see the small space inside the space
shuttle;

12. Space shuttle

High above the Oasis of the earth, your body reflecting,
The dappled zone azure glow of oceans rolling far below,
You are waiting patiently for your final pilgrims to arrive,
There is the space of empty clouds,
Near to the planets , far away from the sun,
The Stardust is sparkling near the shuttle,
Space is full of dark with vaccum;

13. The Malabar coast

In the south, there is the hill with coastal plain,
Lagoons with backwaters , were the great monsoon arrives,
The coast lying narrow coastal plain of Karnataka and Kerala
states,
Were the spices and the coconuts palm lies,
Lots of migratory birds with deep valleys and shallow waterfalls,
With pleasant atmosphere and monsoon strikes at the coast;

14. Keep moving

A time comes when you're strength fails,
Your hope fades, your confidence goes low,
And all The thing is you see yourself, how you are?
On barren island with no men, only palm trees and simple
breeze,
Were no hopes lies , just waves and big ocean that never ends,
Where inner soul go dead , no dream to acquire, at that
moment,
You see yourself, In the water, your face,
You have completely broken, exhausted, tired and you lie helpless
;
With a heartbeat per minute beating like a clock with tick- tok;
You see one ship coming around you, but it flashes light and
continues to go,
The ray of little hope, left like faded lights,
Guilt and sorrows with you;
But noble men told me that after every faded night, the sun will
rise hard to protect you from the storm in your brain, heart and
chest,
Move on, no matters how many months you will take ?
How many weeks you will take??
How many days you will take???

Just do and don't lose your identity in these waves ,
Waves are looking like a dilemma of diamonds in water,
In which you have to pass, go deeper and deeper and suddenly
lost ;
You should be like tides or thunderstorm,
Don't juggle in the nutcracker, be the men of the struggling star
to twinkle bright;
Again bright again bright to the brightest of all ;

15. The moon

I know the valley through it's solitude ,

A brown roads winds towards a mountain crest;

There are gnarly ti-trees dripping sweetness rest;

And grasses bend , too heavily bedowed,

In that still valley, by the still lagoon,

A ruined homestead , for her secret shrine,

Dwells beauty self, half earthly, half divine,

Thrilling I saw her waken to the moon,

In peaks of emeralds the cactus crept;

And there o'ver rafters falling decay,

I saw her in the bamboo trees, were she wore a petals ivory

design dress;

Were the heart is robbed, as she blossomed out like an enlighted

moon,

Were there is no scars but all, things are immaturely perfect;

16. Ladakh

The magical charms of Himalayas,
With rough and rugged terrains;
It holds immense pristine beauty for its beholder;
Thy mystical Lamas where centuries old,
Monasteries have still maintained there charm ;
As a high as a mountain scars, so deep a silence runs within you,
The eyes that speaks the beauty,
A word of rugged valleys, mountains endless hills, and barren
lands ,
The Lake is peaceful and the reflection of that majestic
mountains mesmerized the view
O the valley of Ladakh truly infallible,
The mist of your beauty is unbreakable (unbearable);

17. College life

Stepping into a new life where one faces oneself,
Some consider life is a race, to chase after all,
While other find , it difficult to even tie their shoelace,
Many here care for you,
But you care for a selected few,
Lots of lesiure, lots of pressure, in the midst of which, some search
for treasure;
The greatest invention being the headset,
Without which no one heads are fit,
More sleep, less work, but still feeling tired every other minutes,
Pressure of exam, pressure for life,
Everything gives the lesson to learn;

18. Love after love

The time will come when with elation,
You will greet yourself arriving at your own door, in your own
mirror,
And each will smile at the other's welcome,
And say, sir were eat,
You will love again the stranger who was yourself,
You will love the entity of yourself,
The virtues of your own, the desire the breathe and the
atmosphere;
Which is needed by you;
Be the person, now know the self-care,
The care which will help you to love yourself;

19. I hope you're okay

There's no coming back even if I had want simply your departure
that killed me,
It was your decision to abandon me to leave,
In the midst of chaos and uncertainty you're ,
Decision to choose yourself, when I was most lonely,
To leave me all alone on my own, to freed off world hungery and
thirsty of blood;
The blood of those
I ' ve always loved, my blood;
There are truths that are unspoken,
Only time they surfaced is when my subconscious mind get roped
,
In taking control of consious me who constantly;
Loathing the decision and ignorance of the younger me that has
got me so broken;
My heart it's broken it' soaked in the pool of loneliness;
Open only for something that has awoken inside of me,
The burning desires to keep or writing and fighting the chain of
addiction I ve been trying to break open;

20. The Mountains and you

I have seen the valleys , the rivers and the Orion deer , as you
have guided them,
Your house was near to the nubra valley,
Where old Scottish farm house and nubra flows,
I have seen you in the night at the beautiful full moon,
Where the crescent rays reflects on the beautiful face of moon,
You look gorgeous moon, wearing pashmina of golden green,
I asked the rose where is your scent,
She said " the autumn took it away"
I asked the spring, why the lines on your forehead,
She said it is Noor on the beautiful moon,
I wandered around the hills, the shikhara was my soul as
Arabian nights,
The mountains cliches the soul and moon reflects the spiti;
Snow capped mountains, plentiful wildlife,
Blue lakes, and the dal said more forward gentlemen;
I have seen the rose in the beautiful kashmir,
Roaming in the Gulmarg, passes surrounding with lushy green
grass,
And ethnic beauty with lanterns in the hands,
As the festival celebrates the moon in the bamboo trees:
With pandas, and moose cat and dwindling fireflies;

The rose glimpses her face,
As whole people come to celebrate,
The rose is the beauty angle of an Golden Hour,
Like a moon Of white pearl and magenta red,
With pashmina, looking like thousands of diamonds, will glow,
For your beauty;

21. The rain

There will come rain and the smell of the ground,
And swallows circling with their shimmering sound,
And frogs in the pools, singing at night,
And wild plum trees in tremendous white,
Robin will wear their feathery fire,
Whistling their whims on a low fence – wire,
And noone will know to the war, not one will care at last when
it is done,
The rain which will come and will side out the war,
There will be the new rise of the sun,

22. The country in which I was born

The country in which I was born were the ganga flows,
Were the great Himalayas and the pir Panjal lies,
From the icy glaciers, to Siachen with Misty Greenlands;
In the west the coast lies, in the East of the 7 sister's ,first
The Heaven on earth and god's own country in the same
kingdom,
The beautiful cuckoo sings in East,
The rich gifts of Rainent or grain of gold in the west,
Were the nightingale sings
O Ooty, o blushy ,o glushy
The nature you soak my heart, my country, my love,
Were green and shaded leaves fall,
Of ordered woods and gardens falls,
A land of sweeping plains of ragged mountain ranges, of
droughts and flooding rains,
Underneath the trees there are the flowers,
Sometimes crossing drainage ditches
Between streets you can hear it sing,
I was born in the land of infinity rays;

23. Journey

Today I see the moon, white and excessive,
It's the same as yesterday, same as tomorrow,
But different, never was it so grand so pale,
I tremble as light, trembles on water,
I tremble as light, trembles the water,
I tremble as in eyes tears tremble ,
I tremble as in flesh, the soul knows to tremble,
Oh! The moon has moved her 2 silver lips,
Oh! The moon has told me the 3 ancient words,
"Death ,love and mystery, oh my flesh is finished,
From spent body my soul lifts,
Travel boundless skies,
On the white moon,
The moon shines at the night and journey along with it,

24. Today

If ever there were a spring day so perfect,
So uplifted by a warm intermittent breeze,
That it made you want to throw open all the windows in the
house,
And unmatched the door to the canary's cage,
Indeed , rip the little door from its jamb,
A day when the cool bricks paths and the garden bursting with
peonies,
Seemed so etched in sunlight that you felt like taking,
A hammer to the glass paperweight on the living room end table,
Releasing the inhabitants from their snow covered cottage,
So they could walk out, holding hands and squinting
Into this larger dome of blue and white,
Well , today is just that kind of days,

25. Relatives

When we wake up brushed up by panic,
In the dark our pupils grope for the shape of things we know,
Photons loosed from slits like greyhounds at the track reveal
lights,
Doubleness in their cast shadows,
That stripe a dimmed labs wall particles no more and with a
wave bid all certainties goodbye,
For what sure in a universe that dopplers away like a sirens
midnight cry ? They say,
A flash seen from on and off the hurting train,
Will explain why time dilates like a. Perfect afternoon, predicts
blackhole where parallel lines will meet whose stark horizon even
starlights,
There are the heavy hazards of dusk down,
And if you will see the stars of constellations,
With microscopic and if you look little clear there is a leap with
relativity;

26. New Beginning

To everyone who is struggling is going through difficult time,
Who is struggling and feeling like drowning,
Nothing permanent this will be pass , just like everything else in
life,
No matter how dark it is right now,
No matter how painful it feels , sun will come out again,
It will bring the raise of hope , no matter how dark will be,
No matter how hard will be??
The only reason you can do it is be self believer,
The bad situations will come and go when there will be
happiness, enjoy the moment,
Make new entities, some make new beginning,
The beginning will change your life,
Small steps can make you big forever,

27. Things to Believe

*Trees in general, oak so special, burr oaks that survive fire, in a
particular,*
And the generosity of Apples,
Seeds all of them, carrots like dust,
Winged maple, double beet, peach kernel,
He inevitability of change;
*Frog song in spring cattle lowing on the farm across the hills the
melodies of sad old songs,*
Comfort of savoury soup, sweet iced fruit, the aroma of yeast,
A friend voice, hardwork,
Seasons, bedrock, lilacs,
Moon shadows under the ash groves,
Something breaking through the dawn;

28. How you are??

While lost in song just now, I felt there clear as day and I

wonder if you are still talking in your sleep upside down

quarters,

And countertops and other accidental only I would know,

About apostrophes and timings, the proper order of things and I

along to ask are you setting closer?

Closer the fortune star is waiting for the changing future,

You drop your buds listening the song,

I whistle near house,as I call the one drop can't recognise me,

There were the thoughts sparkling my mind,

Just standed position I Observe you,

In night also, you are too beautiful as Moon,

I felt that you willing to call me,

But in the name of love,I came to see you,

And to ask, How are you??

29. From North to earth

The face of hills splashing the rays of the sun,
With baskets of bronze shouldered trod along the new cement
road,
Not a single child under the shade of a tree,
To wave their parents to eat from the fields,
A river of rust brightly black under the moon,
He heard their heartbeats with the moon with cold rain near the
dawn,
A petals with two flowers and asteral signs,
Near the earth with clementing rose,
Talking to the north with harmony songs,
Roses are red with cliffing clouds, to be asteral as the earth
denotes,

30. In the woods

I found you in the dark forest, were there was teak wood and you
were seen under the big tree,
A tree of shades were the northern stars been enlightened,
Vividly sun was closed in the clouds,
Dark clouds and more rain,
As destiny tries to meet us in the woods,
Were there was nature and you,
Hills were capped with snow, a small pavement were in visible
with mist fog,
A squirrel came from the hole of oak tree,
She took the nuts and moved to home,
A home were everyone is safe, a cuckoo came her voice has
dwelled my heart;
We sat, I am just looking her,
She was praying to get off, from the forests;
But I think let it be the time, can't be changed,
It should stop for while, I should enjoy the nature and just
looking towards you;

31. Five Landscape

One

Green moves through the top of the trees and grows,

Lighter green as it recedes, each of which includes grey, or beyond

them, waning finely while spot absolute it could be an egret or

perhaps crane it edge of the water,

Where it meets as strip of sand,

Two

Lake is waving high with little tides,

With no change in the doons and the forest land,

Wild green grass, sun with flattering clouds in the horizon with

binomial rays,

Three

Forest and green trees fleshy and moist climate,

Rain again, rain again with pity vibes to change,

Regolith of rocks and the grains of small stones carved the crave,

climes of the mountains and the birds eye watching the hunt of

deer by hiding tiger;

Four

A white bird in danger to cry while talking to strangers at

staring the sun and thousands other things,

Five

The air across the valley is slightly hazy,

*Raining through the tin house remain in the groves of trees that
edge a clearing in which stands a single house,*

32. In the woods

I found you, in the dark forests, were there was teak wood and
you were seen under a big tree,
A tree of shades were the northern stars been enlightened,
Vividly sun was closed in the clouds,
Dark clouds and more rain,
As destiny tries to meet us in the woods,
Were there was nature and you
As destiny tries to meet us again, were there is nature and you,
Hills were capped with snow, a small pavements were invisible
with mist fog,
A squirrel came from the hole 9f oak tree ,
She took the nuts and moved to home,
A home were everyone is safe, a cuckoo came her voice has
dwelled my heart,
We both sat, I am just looking her,
She was praying to get off from this forest,
But I think let it be the time, can't be changed,
It should stop for while, I should enjoy the nature and just
looking towards you;

33. Dark matter

With each day I have been writing something,
With each month I have wishing someone,
With each year I am loosing myself,
With each moment I just remember you,
With each year I missed you,
What were the stars? Stars are just a ocean of lights raised high,
Were are you, I am missing you as dark matter;
Were constellations are alone without you;
Were there is nothing to prove;
There is always you and yourself,
But the life seems to be unhappy and sadness,
With your absence of light which Unpasses me ,

34. Within this tree

35. The train

I have missed you in the platform, you had been on another
train,
There is tiny rain drops it realises how we meet in the station;
In these rainy days, we both came on side -by-side,
But still don't you realise, for half an hour,
We sat at railway stations,
In that stations you stared me 2 times,
I noticed and looked up elsewhere as I didn't know,
I looked you but you noticed and looked elsewhere,
There was announcement was made that the train maybe delay
for 2 days due to heavy rain,
We sat till the evening, you start hesitate, and called home, tried
the call for all ;
I seen you panick'd , but you were not in situation to say hold on,
just relax;
And will be okay, with you just relax;
You asked me my name, and I asked you,
We both moved out of station and went to Mall and then hotel,
We eat, we enjoyed, we seen the places,
And after 2 days, we again moved to different destinations,
Were we came from;

I have missed the platforms, the train, and the small rain, in
which the time was spent with you;
It was the time, which was beautiful,
The beautiful time has mesmerized me, the memories with train
and long distance destiny;

36. A letter to child within me

A letter to child within me dear you,
I wish I was more like you,
I wish I could run the streets with orange candy dripping from
my teeth,
I wish I could laugh like no one heard,
I wish I could love without getting hurt,
I wish I could be as lean and thin dear you are still alive within?
Can I hold your hand and be like you for a while,
Can I still be carefree and innocent like a child?
In the child within me, if you are still around tell me how,
You can be found,
Can I go back in time to when I was ten for I wish to be myself
again;

37. You meet me

From the glass of Polaroid motion, I have seen , you, with flower
and carrybags;
You were coming to staircase, were the large hall in the upside ,
As you gleam up in the staircase with roses in your hand,
I see you, you look so beautiful,
As the sea of ocean with deep motions,
As the sea of ocean with deep motions,
You are the motions of thoughts, the thoughts and the expression
which tells me petals are dwells to you,
You are so beautiful that I stopped for a while,
And used to see my heart, it was beating fast
I feel in love, when you meet and talked to you,
You talk like world as horizon to meet;

38. Lectures you Bunked in the schools

*In the chemistry lab, amidst pratical examinations, your hand
run like puppets in a street theatre,
And your life dance with happiest
You see the outer world, is fun with no stress and enjoying the
life,
But you don't Know the struggle outside the world,
While you try to gulp the thick goblets of atomic reactions down
your throat, it will be poetry that will uncork the water bottle
and teach you the meaning of bread,
/ Hanas that hold hands matter more than those that hold test
tubes and get the experiment right/
You are young and you believe in the dictionary definition of
strong,
Strength to you, is buried in the glittering commodities they sell
in retail shops in the name,
You see the life is so easy and all things are going according to
you,
And whole day you have fun, the fun with new everything you
know the maths teacher,
And you didn't go and enjoy the day,*

39. A boy from Afghanistan

If you will see my book read the stories,

I have wrote you will get to know,

There is many incidence and stories where,

If we were get dead and there is no men on land of Afghanistan,

anyone from world can come to our land,

My competitors, cut my heart,tears streamed from my eyes,

O restless one, your heart is stronger than stone,

I weep for you and you laugh at me,

We love the dusty and muddy houses ,

The sand was breezing like a waves,

But the enemy has stolen, our lights,

Everything has gone from the world,

The world become empty, humans become animals,

I stone him with the stones of light tears,

Then I hung my sorrows, in the gallons like Mansour,

Like those who have been killed by infindels,

I count my heart, as one of the martyr,

It might have been the bitter taste of your memory,

Life is little joy and happiness here, it's bazaars and Shop are full

of goods,

Life were so much lost individual that there is no affection of
brother and brother,
There is bodies which lies here,
There is knowledge so great that they have drilled oil in the depth
of oceans,
But even there knowledge doesn't give any reputation,
I see there knowledge doesn't give any reputation,
I see there is more faults and virtues with my own eyes;
I see the women's were not allowed to move alone anywhere
But what can I say?
My heart doesn't have any patience to bear this,
Everyday a new death and new martyr,
I know, the black, black mountains,
I know the desert, and it's problem
My home is in mountains my village is in mountains and I live
in mountains,
I know the black ditches,
I always carry rocket launcher with me,
I know the hot trenches, I always ambush the enemy,
I know the war, conflicts and disputes ,
I know the pamir's canyon, I walk it through day and night,
There were the slits and hidden cannons,
I know the caves werethe stay, and hide to attack,
I know the enemy to the neighbourhood
Where they hide under the tall mountains,
To attack and kill them secretly, this is my story, you will see my
book,

This is my story you will see my book,
If you will get,

40. Monsoon Begins

Drops of life on mortal earth, new green lush had taken birth,

Soothing waves of true enchant, came like box of eternal grant,

Scorching rays in wildest face smiled as a devil in fiery race,

Helpless lives in deep torment;

Played in lines of dead red paint,

Sweaty skins and stinky hairs;

Beyond all pleadings beyond the prayers,

Miles of agony, miles of grief, then came the waves of true relief,

I felt a drop and two or more I felt them on a door,

I heard the floating chunk to lark,

Blunt yet soothing, sweet a bark

They spikes the rain and spike of wind,

I heard them through my restless mind,

I knew by then in signals true, black has captured the searing

blue,

41. I was waiting for you

*I was sitting there whole evening in the hope of seeing sunset
together,
And I believed you got late, struck in traffic,
I sat there alone holding my thoughts and feelings for you,
I sat there looking at my phone every minute, waiting for a text
or call from you,
But you never showed up,
I don't know the reason and neither,
I don't know where you are right know,
But one thing I know, I won't be able to sleep the way is use to,
rest of my life,
I won't be able to laugh the way I use to, rest of my life,
I won't trust anyone the way I use to, rest of my life,
Sunset are not beautiful when were you;*

42. About pain

In the deep sky, in million miles apart,
The sun still finds way, to bring light to the moon, and you
expect me, to leave you in the darkness,
In the deep sky, even though million miles apart,
You think that the day will whipe out,
And there will be the dark encroachment,
Make you feel pain, but in the deep sky million miles apart,
The sun still finds way, to bring light to the moon,
That is you,
And you will never been afraid, with the lovely sun,

43. About Emptiness

Maybe you will never know why I never said the word,
Why I pushed you away
Why I buried my feelings
Why I chained my heart and headed skin,
Under the deepest sea, coz, I couldn't allow you to drown,
In the never ending chaos, which was only mine,
Maybe you will never know why I never said the word,
Maybe you will never know the secret behind the emptiness
The Emptiness which is never about the love,
The Emptiness which is never been told you,
Forever by me, or said glimpses are there for you,

44. About dreams

You think your dreams are dying but here is the truth,
Dreams that never dies,
They are simply leaving you,
When dream grows tired they leave homes, there destiny and
there path,
They believe they deserve better coz, dreams loved ones , more
than thinkers;
Dreams respires in your blood and body,
Dreams are home of thought,needs the place to be evolved,
Needs the space to be grown,
Dreams never ever die
They remain with you, if you care or handled it with softly,
Just relax, think about it,
You will see it never dies it is always with you forever and ever,

45. About Hope

We are traped in Ocean's, trying but failing to reach remarkably,
We are just two people yet holding hope
We are just two people get trapped,
We are just in nusiance of the hope,
To get rid of the traped oceans,
From the darkness of the room, were darkness and no path to
found,
There is the rays of Amber, which does not know the darkness,
But hope brings light to the home,
Hope brings the people get rid out from the ocean,

46. Rain

There will come soft rain and the smell of the ground, blooms

And swallows circling with there shimmering sound,

And frogs in the pools, singing at night,

And wild plum trees in tremulous white,

Robins will wear their feathery clothes,

Whistling their whims on a low fence wire,

And no one will know the war , will care at last when it is done,

No one would mind, neither bird nor trees,

If mankind perished utterly,

And spring herself, when she woke at dawn,

Would scarcely know that we're gone,

And the rain will gently see and make you feel that she will come

again,

47. The Night Eclipse

That dusk wasn't a silent one at all,
Yet, the sweetest one, dazzling walking across the corridor,
Wisps of lights and shadows, out there were screams and cries,
Like masquerading the Lullabies eyes seeking the embedded stars,
In a chest of gauzy clouds, and there as a glimmer flashing above
the whole sky,
The moon grew a perfect gold orb,
Overhanging the dark purple paper sky,
Night was drunk in Lights, till it crashed to kiss the land,
Burning rocks splashing everywhere breaking loose fountains of
red,
And the most beautiful tragedy shined,
With blood and fire roses,

48. The Arabian Nights

When the breeze of a joyful dawn blew free,
In the silken sail of infancy, the tide of time flow'd back with me,
The forward flowing tide of time,
And sheeny summer morn, adown the Tigris I was born ,
The Bagdad was shrines of fretted gold,
The treachery of arms and weapons found,
The Lake and the mountains were formed,
Were there is the new civilization grow'd ,
The nights in Arabia was as old as fifty pounds,

49. Hunger

I have seen the people who are letting there days by single breed ,
I have seen the people with no penny
No food, no shelter, with tired guts,
Untidy clothes, and unblissed chaos,
They spend there life in complete dark
With nothing to eat for living that hunger which is dead end,
Which cause human being to feel insecure about health,
I see the old men, there was nobody to help,
The men, the people around them were noone,
Hunger a stage of destruction some die, some struggle, some feed,
some lost,
Life for struggle to get away from Hunger,

50. Hymn of Autumn

September is coming soon,
Beautiful morning without a fuss,
The crisp of golden sky, with sun rays straight into my eyes,
Light summer tops and shorts now pilling up in a cupboard,
Warm sweaters scarves boots out of the closest especially the
hoods,
Ice cream is no longer my favourite, yup,
But love to curl cold hands round hot tea cup,
Sweet beautiful Autumn carrying gold,
Wearing the loveliest smile, lightening my soul,
Leaves starts changing colours from green,
To burn orange, dark red,
What a beautiful scene?
The crimson leaves dancing and falling,
They fill the empty street, beautiful sprawling,
Wonderous beauty in every direction oh our lord's perfection,
They fall yes, but they will rise again for sure following his
direction,

51. Hawa Mahal

The Royal Ladies eye behold , the scene that us to unfold
The procession just outside the Hawa Mahal,
She looks from one of 953 windows,
The red and pink sandstone of Mahal,
With marvellous it's structures,
With porthole has Miniature windows,
And carved sandstone grills, finals and dome,
She is rajput by heart and family, and invardly thanks maharaja
Sawai Singh for intricate piece of art,
Constructed in 1799,
The soothing air blew from the windows,
Out of there all kinds of people old, young fancy, simple,
They see the people from the "Jharokas"
The red sandstone and unique honey comb,
Structures have created by Ustad lal,
The queen have the stories to tell,
The royal palace for summer of all times,

52. The princess

The petals have bloom, the sepals have turned down,
The stigma emerges inside the flower,
The rose have seen the smile,
The mountains have leaved the clouds,
To see a beautiful girl in the palace,
The knights are rescuing, the king know her princess,
The kingdom know there princess moon folds in the clouds,
As princess in her bed,
She is so beautiful that never been explained in words,
The princess who is shine to her Kingdom and bravery within
her,
Never forgotten by all,

53. Siberia

A golden train were the tons of gold was carried out,

During world war 2 it was the knight 7 by the name ,

Was going from Moscow to Siberia,

Moscow the city of jewels as flourishing,

But the time of industry revolution was there,

With new technosavy world were the train was the revolution of

the age,

There was the wars and revolution was started,

And at the moment there was the general commander of the

army,

Who had ordered there officers,

To shift the gold from the Moscow to the place were noone reach

The place were nobody know in the tunnel no.8

There was tunnels during the war,

Train reached with 89 containers and sub 46 containers get

attached,

Reached the land full of snow,

No sun, for 6 months and bliss of snow and lie,

The trained moved to tunnels were there was huge space to shift

the gold,

The gold which is enough to buy the nation,

ATHARVA HANMALWAR

Infrozen tanks inside the pond, covered with petrochemical high resistance , still there is tunnel,

54. The Valiant Maharana Pratap

Hills

Turned to red blood and saffron turbaned heads,

Guerrilla warfare, so rana choose to save his men with swords

and bows from guns

Akbar's forces couldn't single out Pratap to capture him alive or

dead;

Rana beat retreat into the hills,

But 2 Mughals pursued him for head for them to be awarded

with royal gifts,

The chetak first time breathed his last on Rana's Pratap

And shed a master tears on his closing eyes,

The loss of all his ferocious fighters in sanguinary battles fought

often,

Made Rana grievous and he exiled himself,

Into the desert , with remaining men,

The lion of Mewar defied again and rallied his men to regain his

fort,

Akbar ceased from fertile wars with rana,

And turned his ire to the west of North,

Rana ruled in peace to ease of all,

In his last time in peace at nebulous vision,

He saw his horse and his soul not bow to Delhi and flew up

mounting chetak ;

55. Battle of Delhi

*These was the time of 1757, were at Northern side a strange
rohillas coming for the battle,
From another side, there Marathas who are the brave warrior of
India,
Najib-ud – daula who was under Afghan suzeranity,
And pay master of Mughals army,
The capital was under the control of rohilla and consequences of
the 4th invasion of India by Ahmed Shah Abdali,
Abdali came and capture the Mughal emperor under home
arrest,
After return of Abdali in 1957, he reinstalled Alamgir -2 as
titular ahead of Delhi throne,
The mughal emperor requested Marathas to get rid of Abdali
from Delhi,
The Marathas promised to win the battle with lion
roar,.Maratha dispatched 40,000 troops to attack Delhi,
The Marathas encamped opposite to the red fort, on other side of
yamuna river,
The Battle started on 11 August 1757,
On one side Marathas headed by Raghunath rao and Malharrao
Holkar;
On another side Najib -ud- Daula and rohilla Afghans,*

The war was started intensely, the warriors troops and heavy
artilleries prevents the Marathas to enter city,
But Maratha never Bow head , nor give the empire,
Even the pride beheaded, Neither bow, nor give ;
The war was lasted upto two weeks of intense fight,
Finally Najib surrendered to the Marathas,
At last Maratha won by heavy victory,
And demand 50 Lakh rupees and said never to look back again
to India;

56. Marathas – The Great

A life, history, journey, rival Was born on the fort of shivneri,
Brought joy and glory with him, he named after the god shiva,
He brought under the watchful eye of tutelage of his mother,
She told him stories from ramayan and Mahabharata and
kindled in the flame of freedom,
In very young age became brave and warrior with wisdom,
Learned the ethics and supported the women,
He won his 1st fort ' Torna' when he was 16
He fought against the Mughals, Adil shah, Nizamshah,
Qutubshahi , siddi johar and the cunning Brahmins,
He was devout Hindu, but respect to all religions,
The man who opposed forced conversions,
The Pioneer of guerrilla warfare tactics,
Revived ancient Hindu political traditions and encouraged the
use of Sanskrit and Marathi,
His soldiers was valour as the shivaji known by Mawala ,
They were expert climbers , guerrilla tactics and expert hunters,
Shivaji was the ruler of navy, in ocean,
He founded his hindu kingdom "Hindavi swarajya "
Moral virtues was exceptional high and incredible,
Won, constructed and repaired forts more than 300,
He was his enemy's nightmare and main dread,

His skills as an administrator was legendary,
When he won the forts and established himself crown as
"Chhatrapati shivaji "
When he walk the Mughal ruler threatened, by his fear,
When he roar , they fear as dead hunt,
He comes as a nightmare and fears for unjust one,
Almighty of all legendary king who worship after Lord Shiva
and named as "Raja dhiraj chatrapati shivaji Maharaj "
A clan of Bhonsle family, who is fearless, fruitful and wisemen, a
saffron flag with pride;

57. The Night in Museum

The night was peace with chaos,

It was the museum were the dinner and antic drawing were

placed,

In the frames of mirror with safe handle,

The auction was started for the painting which is unique in

their styles,

The night were the flashing lights and beautiful diamonds have

been seen,

Were the history told it was from india,

The Nadir Shah robbed it and taken to turkey,

From turkey passed to Phillipines and then to Britain,

From Britain it finally reached to the France,

Were there was around 1,000 of artistic frame, and much more

has amazed all,

The museum were seen the species of 100 year old butterfly,

insects and bone of dinosaurs,

The hall was silent with wihspers of starlight which ultimate my

path while casting shadows in the night,

As I walk I realise the art all around me was Marvel and beauty

surrounds me,

There was the floor which was upside down,

With unique engineering of past,

58. Life and death

We must remember that we are were travellers of life,
On a journey to Home, that nothing will matter in the end,
For everything is chaos, except laugh,
Life and death you, revive you from the dead, non living,
The non living which is unsustainable path have no virtues,
nothing only dead,
Were family, friends and all goes to vain,
Nothing left within fraction of second goes to dead,
The part is critical but sure the death is for all,
As life is to few,
So life and death is part of Human being to roll;

59. Universe

The world will disappoint you, universe will not trust you
The whole race of life, will make you fade,
But matter of universe will spell and create path for you,
You, just have to believe in the spell of universe,
Listen, with care, and hold your breathe
Do in and out
Just relax, yourself and get out all your darkness out,
Enlight your body with chaos around you,
The beauty of sea, the breeze of the wind,
And the freshness of nature,
Just feel it, you feel better not disappointed;

60. About Heartache

You won't born with heartbreak, you won't die with one, then
why live with it;
These world so much to offer, you deserve better, except, allow
embrace allow;
Just close textbook of your life, open your mind see outside the
environment ,
Were you will know heartache can't dissolve your innersoul??

61. A man who had Gifted you all

A man who had Gifted you all,
All the joy and happiness to all,
Carrying big responsibility tries every possible things in his
arsenal,
Still get questioned for his abilities,
He is strong, invincible go and look at him at night,
He is too vulnerable,
When he's hope is gone,
He has nothing to loose,
He can drink for his sadness and sorrows,
But there isn't such strong booze,
Nothing in his life, just his love and family,
Nobody to bother about him
But he worries about all,
Shows his feelings to all,
But never share emotions to all,
He deserves most, but noone to give his honour,
But he don't fight for his respect, at all,
But still a man who gifted you all,

62. The ocean

The sea, is calm tonight, the tide is full, the moon lies fair,
Upon the straits, on the Marina trench of light,
Gleams is gone, the cliffs of Mumbai,
With tranquil bay,
Where sea Meets the moon – blanched land,
Listen! You hear the waves which grating roar,
Of pebbles which the waves, draw back and fling,
There was the Musk deer with enlightened twigs,
Near the sand, were the ocean starts,
There was the raft, yacht alongside of the deer,
The night was spend with barbeque near the bay of ocean,

63. The Lilies

I bought fifteen white lilies for my friend,

When I learned she might have cancer,

Easter was gone, the trumpet were wilted, plants crooked with

roots, bound in pots,

I dug them in the garden, knowing they would not bloom for

another year,

All the summer the stalks stood like ramshackle posts

While I waited for results,

By Autumn the stalks had flopped down

The earth remained bare, rhizomes shrunken below the frost

line,

Spring shoots appeared in bright, green skins and lilies bloomed

in July, their waxed trumpets pure white,

Dusting gold pollen, they are popping up again,

I wait a ceremony, for lilies to open, for the serpentine length of

the garden to bloom,

I took out all the Lilies with red, white yellow colour and gifted

to her,

She diagnosed by doctor said, you are at last stage of brain

cancer,

I have seen the affection of praise before the ICU room,

And said to God for blessings to her,

Give life and make happy to her family,

64. The train to Rajasthan

Long before you see train, the track sing and tremble, long before

you know direction

Train come from hum announces it soon arrive,

As arrives we sit to the window place,

Were you see the trees and mountains,

There is the mountains and as the city passes,

You see the dry places and thorny herbs along with forts and

palaces,

You see the sky crapers, some use to sell there food in stalls,

The stalls were you will get drinking water,

As the train starts see the tree passes by,

The bird sings the song and the puppet dance,

Ploughed field,

The desert, fold mountains kumbargarh and so many things,

The rajasthan the land of imperial things and culture the

customs have shown the power endemity and closure exposure of

monuments and architecture is truly marvellous in these modern

world,

65. The god's own country

Where the palm grove abound, tall the trees grow,
Fertile and adorn paddy fields, emerald glow,
Where 44 rivers, which embelishes her perennial greenery,
The moist landscape with green trees,
Crystal clear beaches and coconut palm along side the road,
Which smells the ethnicity of loess,
Where the rain starts from the Malabar coast,
Cochin, Malabar,canara to travancore spread widely;
There is abundance of flora and fauna with exotic varities,
With patches of green land and nature abode,
The lighthouse beach, varkala beach and coffee gardens
At the hill top were you see the contour farming of coffee,
Arcanut with lushy trees and houseboats along with temples,
rituals ,
The country is rich in nature and spices,

66. The fort in the forest

There was deep forest with wild animals,
Tiger roar, loudly alone hide in the trees,
We moved, in the deep forest were we saw waterfall and big
banana trees,
The banana trees and then we move to the middle of forests,
Were all kinds of animals stay in the home,
Near the home there was a mountain,
We raised towards mountains, as we reached to the mountains,
Saw the fort which was ancient in origin,
Were the great battles were fought,
To free the kingdom for wisdom,
To free the kingdom for wisdom,
To free the nation from the dead pound people,

67. Towards the south

Towards the south were rituals and high tradition followed
Land with diversity and faith in God
The gardens and toad croons a tender sky-blue
The nightingale that love has bruised sings in the beaches,
There is the elephants and biggest spices hubs you get,
You will see the orchards and green trees,
The world's biggest diamond was formed in Andra Pradesh,
Were the land of rich heritage and greenery,
The south with sunny face
Cotton and the moon;
Warmth, earth, warm sky the sun, the stars the magnolias scent
in the south;

68. Your heart is your home

Your heart is your home a home were
You find all the answer to those questions that makes you
uncertain in the path you're going,
A destination that makes you feel in the essence of happiness,
peace and satisfaction, like the moon,
A home feel at all, the stars,
Like the lighthouse, a destination to all,
Those wandering ships, and your heart,
To its forever companion you,
Coz, darling as life means to follow your heart,
That follows you endlessly;

69. The Daffodils

We have seen the beautiful daffodils grown,
As yet the early raising sun , it grows from bunches of leaves,
It shines with drop of fresh Water and sunlight,
With muse of light and the pearls of morning dew,
The wood get Pringles the cuckoo enchanted,
O the Daffodils, you have been grown we celebrate the joy with
you,
You are harbinger of nature,
You are persona of the stream you are the lakes of the dream,
You are the pie of the cake, you are the fruits of the shake,
With daffodils of farm and I will gift you from my heart;

70. Feelings

Some feelings make up everything, in the ocean called life,
We are sailing in it everyday to find ourselves,
The feelings are reciprocal and again comes to us,
Which can'tbe expressed among all,
The heart is so soft to attach with another one is so easy,
So feelings can be shared, adopt and leaved with us forever,

71. Somedays

Somedays we feel as if we are lost falling down,
Deeper ,no matter how hard to try
Every night we think of the butterflies,
That made our days beautiful losing a part,
Leaving apart ourself as if we are masked , all the time,
Traveling at the edge of doubtfulness,
And moving and changing the heart that's always been your
partner,
I thought I was lost of this darkness,
Falling into the dreams that are just as illusions fading myself to
find
Something I m not sure of but all again and again
No matter where I go I found was me,

72. The dark light

We spend our lives running away from the dark towards the
light,
Hoping the light will lead the way,
Hoping the light will show us the path,
Hoping the light will guide us home,
But what if we are heading into wrong direction,
What if the light doesn't see us through?
What if the light is nothing but an Illusion?
But the thing about light is it blind us,
We only see what it want us to see
And often it isn't what we want to be?
And yet
We never embrace the dark we deny it's very existence even
though we know,
It exists everywhere even within us midnight

73. Waiting on the road, looking for sign

My heartbeat fastened when I saw her for the first time,
She looked like a star the way she did shine,
The only thing I can dream about was she being mine,
She was ruling my mind, all night, all day,
There was lot on my mind, but I can't spill and say,
The love I had for her was so pure and profound
Everything now is about her, everything that's around,
Her hand in my hand and miles to walk,
Chit-chatting all day, but yet so much to talk,
A glance of her face and it's brightens up the day,
She felt with a smile when I wanted her to stay,
The world full of happiness and everything so new,
You've already decided that she's the one made for you,
The dreams were turning true but deep down the truth you've
Knew,
It's love for sure, but it's to good to be true,
She wasn't meant to be yours, but your love for her was true,
She was your only ones, there never was a 2,
You have to lock yourself and throw away the key,
Coz , it's sad but true, 1ˢᵗ love never meant to be true,

74. The pigeon

In the twilight of dusk, a pigeon flew into my porch,
And perched gracefully on the wooden railing,
The clock struck the hour of loneliness, I in my wicker chair, sat
Still darkness spoiled from the pigeon beady eye,
Like ink on paper, as light played tricks in the filament,
We communed in silence as it head back and forth
In silent understanding, indispositions of the heart are perhaps,
universally understood, for they show,
Like wrinkles with age, and slowly the moon appeared,
Like objects appears on entering a dark room,
After light its encounter with the sun as transient as mine with
the pigeon,
Which fluttered it's wings in farewell and vanished into the
night leaving maybe;

75. The constancy of change

All winter I waited for snow, but what I got was the monotony
of sunshine, that sweet warmth,
Giving like a faithful lover,
And when it fell, I could only watch like a fanatic witnessing a
miracle,
Until it melted away into little streams that flowed down
winding mountain roads,
I realized then, our constant thirst,
For change, that we're desperate for it as politicians for votes,
corporate slaves for weekends, or
Caged birds for freedom,
Show a man one of the 7 Wonders, of the world, each day for
months,
And he will surely begin to wonder what makes it so special such
is the a version to repetition, the yearning for change,
Now if, had snowed after week, wouldn't I have wished for some
sunshine;

76. Hummingbird

A hummingbird flights from twigs to twigs on a tree by the
window, unperturbed with an indifference as enviable as yours
neighbour riches,
It does not worry, like us about all that can be worried about,
You won't find it perched alone on a window still, staring into
nothingness
Or dreaming of gold plated nests on the greenest trees with
breathe taking views,
It won't have any wild ambitious of becoming the greatest
hummingbird, that ever hummed or the cancerous fear,
Of ending up a nobody in a life,
And I m preety sure no one's seen a heartbroken hummingbird
weeping on the end of branch with cartwheeling in the air with
joy,
No, it's just us , it just us with this recurring habit,
Of complicating things, rooted in conformity,
Like the tree that this bird alighted On seeking answers with
outstretched hands, fingers like these slender boughs,
These slender boughs that quiver faintly as the little bird take off,
And I can't help but imagine hummingbird parents waiting for
their child wing , crossed , Scowling at the poor soul for being
late once again,

And the little one, with it's heart racing, anticipating the banal
punishment of being grounded for a week,
Now wouldn't be a strange;

• 89 •

77. The king's Dinner

A royal men, with royal palace, customed by high tradition and
luxury life;
A magnificent attire held high, with every adminstration leads
with truth;
There is the high nobles, and chief
With power of crown, to rule the nation;
The king though, have the special dinner,
The dinner which consists of delicious and tasty food,
Consists of varities of authentic and hygienic one,
The food is served by 180 servants,
From making, cooking, testing and verified,
Processed towards the king,
There is more appetite and have moan delite cake,
With royal treatment;

78. Flight

Oh! I have slipped surely above bonds of earth,
In the clouds of silver wings, danced skies,
Sunward I have climbed, and joined the tumbling mirth;
Of sun split clouds, and done a hundred things;
You have not dreamed of wheeled and soared swung,
High in the sunlight silence of meadows,
How ring there, I ve chased the shouting wind along and flung,
My eager craft through footless halls in air,
Up the long delirious, burning blue
I ve topped the winds swept heights with grace,
Where never lark nor even eagle flew
And , while with silent lifting mind I ve trod,
The flight, have given the wings,
The wings, which matures the world,

79. Never Believe

We never believe that there is someone behind us who and we'll
being,
In the life we're traveling there are lots of glittering stars in the
stars we meet everyday but when the sunrises,
None of them, appears in our sky,
But there are some twinkling stars twinkle for us,
No matter what place were in;

80. Success

*Success is timespans, it is amount of time passes between you
waking up with an idea and you being able to work on the idea,
The worst feeling in the world is waking up with an idea and
knowing that no one is willing to listen to it yet,
If meet people who will listen to your stuff even though they
know it's not going anywhere, but just for the love of the idea,
And one day when that time span between idea and execution is
done to its very minimum is when you have to work your hardest
and bring those people in save your ideas and remember the
people,*

Young Writers Group

Young Writers Group (YWG.OFFICIAL) is an organisation which is working to help writers in showcasing their work in front of vast number of readers . We offers a budget friendly packages to our writers. We are working as a writer's helping society. You can have a talk with us regarding publishing your book on our instagram :@YWG.OFFICIAL

Or you can drop your mail on ywg.co.in@gmail.com

Else you can also contact us on following numbers

Akash: 7404390981

Aashika: 9634644516